BOOKS BY JOAN ELMA RAHN
ILLUSTRATED BY GINNY LINVILLE WINTER

*Grocery Store Botany*
*How Plants Travel*
*Seeing What Plants Do*
*More About What Plants Do*
*How Plants Are Pollinated*
*The Metric System*

# THE METRIC SYSTEM

# THE METRIC SYSTEM

*Joan Elma Rahn*

*Illustrated by Ginny Linville Winter*

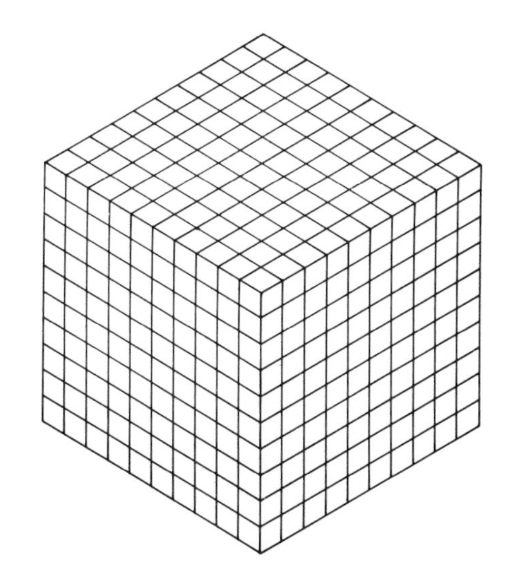

ATHENEUM
*New York 1976*

Library of Congress Cataloging in Publication Data

Rahn, Joan Elma, 1929- The metric system.
SUMMARY: Explains the principles and
uses of the metric system.
1. Metric systems—Juvenile literature.
[1. Metric system] I. Winter, Ginny Linville. II. Title.
QC92.5.R34 389'.152 75-29445
ISBN 0-689-30510-9


Published simultaneously in Canada by
McClelland & Stewart, Ltd.
Manufactured in the United States of America
by The Book Press, Brattleboro, Vermont
First Edition

*To Spencer Grimshaw*

# Contents

# THE METRIC SYSTEM

# Introduction

If you had two boards of different lengths and wanted both of them to be the length of the shorter one, how would you decide where to cut the longer one? The easiest thing to do might be to lay the boards side by side and with a pencil draw a line on the longer one at the place corresponding to the length of the shorter one. Then you would cut along the line. You would not have to know exactly how long the short board is in order to cut another one like it. You would just use the short board as a *measure* by which to judge the length of the new piece.

Suppose, now, that the short board is part of a fence at the bottom of a steep hill and that you have the long board in the basement of your home at the top of the hill. Let's also suppose that the long board is so heavy that you do not want to carry it all the way down to the fence and back. Then you might take a string and a pencil down to the fence. You could make two marks on the string to indicate the length of the board and bring the string back to your basement. You could stretch the string along the board with one mark at one end of the board, and then you would cut the board at the place corresponding to the other mark. In this case, you would be using the length of string between the two marks as the measure by which to determine the length of the new board (and you would be using the short board as a measure to determine the appropriate distance between the two marks on the string).

Now let us suppose that you are not going to cut the board yourself, but that a friend who lives a long distance across town has the long board and will cut it for you. You might take the marked string to him, but perhaps you don't want to travel that far. You could mail the marked string to him, but perhaps that will take too much time. If your friend had a measure already marked to the correct length, you could just telephone him and tell him to use that measure. Actually, most people do have just such a measure. A tape measure is a good example. A tape measure, however, is marked to indicate not just one length, but many. If you and your friend each have a tape measure, all you have to do is to lay your tape measure along the board in the fence to determine the *exact* length you want the new piece to be. Then you can telephone your friend and tell him the length of the board he is to cut. He will lay his tape along the board, find the mark on the tape measure that indicates the exact length you give him, and mark the board for cutting.

A long time ago, probably before recorded history, people realized how convenient it would be if everyone were to have his own measures; then people could tell each other how long something was or how long they wanted something to be. The first measures that people used probably were things they had with them all the time—parts of the body, their feet, for instance. In the English system of measures and in the customary system in the United States, which is based on the English system, the foot is still a unit of measure. Of course, we usually don't use our feet to measure things now, but you probably have a ruler that is one foot long. People once also used their hands to measure things. We rarely use the hand as a measure today, but the height of horses is still given in hands. The inch originally was the length of the segment at the tip of the thumb. The yard was the distance from the tip of the middle finger of an outstretched arm to the tip of the nose. Of course, there were other units of length based on other parts of the body, but just these few should be enough to show you how convenient this method of measuring can be. Unless you were to lose parts of your body in some terrible accident, you would always have your measuring instruments with you. You couldn't forget them or leave them behind, and because you don't have to buy them, they don't cost anything.

Although this system is convenient, it is not accurate, for people come in different sizes, and each person in just one family might have somewhat different inches

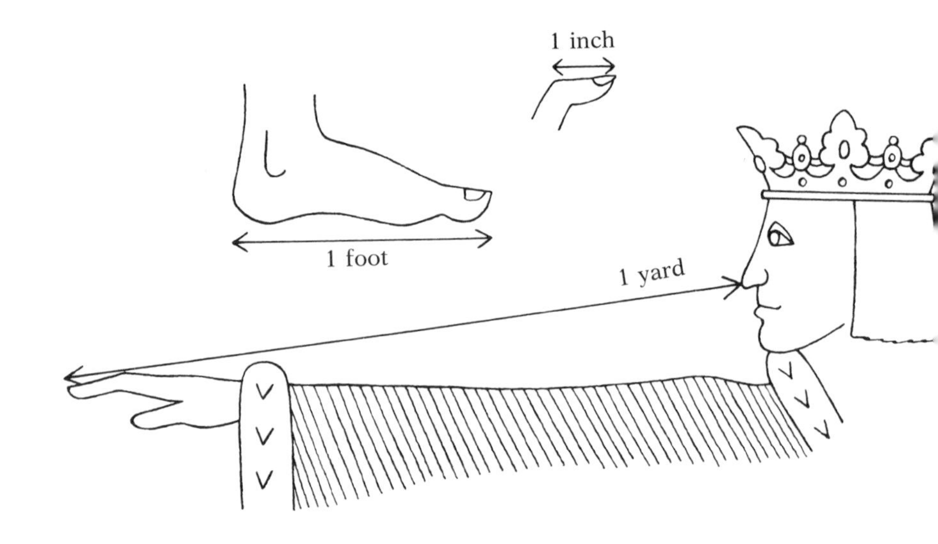


or yards or feet. People realized that it might be better to have *standard* yards and inches and other units of measurement; that is, there would be one yard for everyone, one inch for everyone, and so on. About a thousand years ago, King Edgar of England decreed that the yard would be equal to the distance from the end of *his* nose to the end of the middle finger of his outstretched arm. This yard, based on his body and his body alone, was to be the standard yard throughout the country. Later kings sometimes changed the length of the yard—usually to make it conform to the lengths of their arms—but the standard yard in their time was based on just that one person's arm. King Edgar also established that the foot would be equal to the length of 36 barleycorns (kernels of barley) taken from the middle of the ear and laid end to end.

This system was more accurate than the previous one, for now there was only one length for the foot. Barleycorns might vary in size, but using only those taken from the middle of the ear made for greater uniformity than using barleycorns chosen at random. Furthermore, even if a few of the 36 barleycorns were a little smaller than most of them, there probably were a few that were a little longer, and this evened out the difference fairly well. It might not be perfect, but it was better than having everyone use his own foot.

Of course, this new system was not so convenient as using parts of your own body. The king certainly was not going to let everyone measure the distance from his nose to his fingertips; and even if he did, it would be much too inconvenient for most people to travel perhaps many miles to see him. If you didn't happen to have any barley around the house, determining the length of a foot might be troublesome, too.

Overcoming problems like these is not difficult, however. If the king submitted to just one measurement, the distance from his nose to his fingertips could be measured and recorded on a stick, and the stick could be cut to just that length. This stick then would be a standard yardstick. Copies could be made from it (as in our first example of cutting one board to match another in length), and these copies could be distributed throughout the country, perhaps one to each town. Then someone in each town could make more copies from that copy and sell them to whoever wanted to buy them. In the same way, one set of 36 barleycorns could be used to make one standard one-foot ruler, and then copies could be made from that standard ruler.

Each time someone makes a copy, he may make it just a little too long or too short. Therefore a copy made from a copy made from a copy could have a greater error in it, but yardsticks and one-foot rulers made this way were good enough for everyday purposes.

The length of a foot could be marked on a yardstick,

so it could be used to measure feet as well as yards. An inch was made equal to the length of three barleycorns ($\frac{1}{12}$ of 36) laid end to end, and that distance could be marked on rulers and yardsticks, too.

Inches, feet, and yards are not the only units of length in the customary system of measuring length. For example, there are rods, furlongs, statute miles (used on land), and nautical miles (used at sea). There are also units of length used for special purposes. Surveyors, for example, measure distances in chains (66 feet) and links (7.92 inches).

In other countries, different units of length were adopted. In Thailand, for example, the *wa* is approximately 80 inches long, the *kup* 10 inches, and the *nin* $\frac{10}{12}$ of an inch. In Japan, the *shaku* is just a little less than 12 inches long, and the *cho* equals 360 shaku. In some places, a given unit may have more than one length; in India, for instance, the *guz* is 27 inches in Bombay, 33 inches in Madras, and 36 inches in Bengal.

These are only a few examples of units of length. Throughout the world there are hundreds of units for measuring length, area, volume, weight, temperature, and time—just to mention some quantities that are likely to interest us in our everyday lives. Many crafts, professions, or fields of scientific endeavor have their own particular quantities—like electric currents, energy, or force—that require their own units of measurement.

One disadvantage of the customary system of measuring lengths—and of many other systems as well—is that it is based on more than one unit for each quantity to be measured. In the case of length, there was one definition for the yard and another for the foot, for instance. It doesn't matter if we are talking about the length of a person's foot or of the length of 36 barleycorns in a row; in either case, the foot is a basic unit and the yard is another basic unit. Often when you have two or more basic units for measuring a given quantity they do not fit together well. For instance, the distance from the tip of my nose to the tip of the middle finger of my outstretched arm is almost exactly 36 inches—a yard as we know it today. My feet are only $9\frac{3}{4}$ inches long. Now if I were to use my outstretched arm and one of my feet as standards for a yard and a foot, respectively, then there would be $3\frac{9}{13}$ feet in a yard and not 3 feet exactly. The 36-barleycorn foot probably was a much better fit, but most likely it did not fit *exactly* three times into King Edgar's yard. When situations like this arose, the problem was solved by making one of the units a little longer or a little shorter so that one could fit into the other a whole number of times. Over the years many of our units of measurement have been redefined to make them fit better with others.

Another problem with many systems of measurement is that large units are divided into smaller units by many different numbers. For instance, there are 1760 yards in a statute mile, 3 feet in a yard, 12 inches

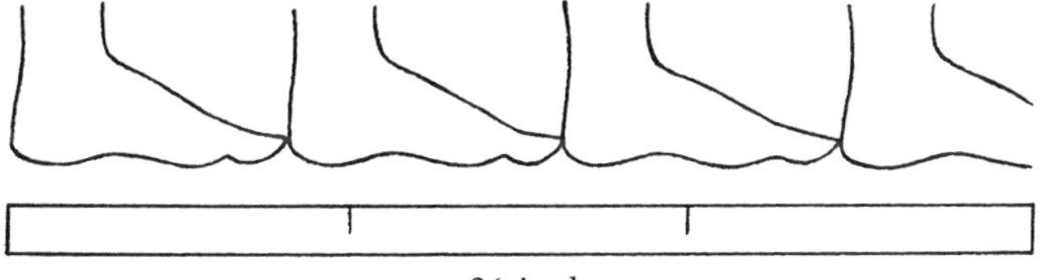

36 inches

in a foot, and the inches in your ruler probably are divided into 8 or 16 smaller units. There are 4 quarts in a gallon and 2 pints in a quart. There are 16 tablespoons in a cup and 3 teaspoons in a tablespoon. There is no way a stranger to our system could guess how many tablespoons there are in a cup. In fact, many persons using the system don't even know. It is just something you must memorize. In fact, you must memorize the entire system if you want to know it.

There must be something better, and there is.

# 1 The Metric System

In 1799 France adopted a system of measurements that avoided many of the problems of other systems. It was called the metric system. It proved so popular that nearly all the nations of the world have adopted it or are in the process of doing so. Scientists the world over, even in nonmetric countries, use it. As this book is being written, the United States is the only major country that has not committed itself to the metric system. Even so, Americans make some use of the metric system, and we hear it used more and more. At the 1972 Olympic Meetings in Munich, Mark Spitz swam the 100-meter freestyle event in 51.2 seconds, thus setting one of several records in men's events. Many photographers, both professional

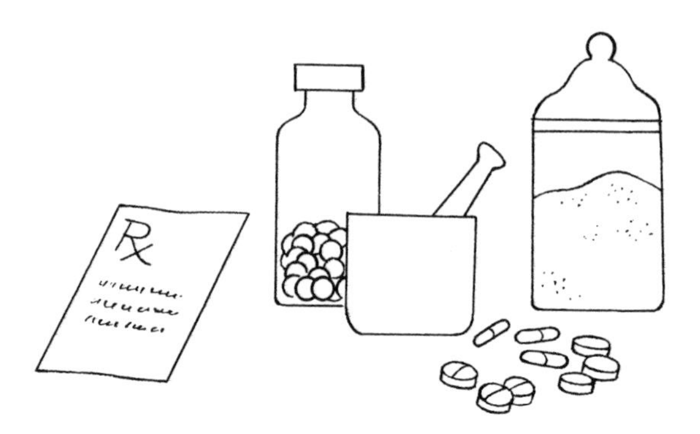


and amateur, use a 35-millimeter camera, which takes 35-millimeter film. The focal lengths of the lenses are also expressed in millimeters. Physicians write prescriptions in metric units, and the pharmacists who fill them use metric instruments to measure or weigh the items in the prescriptions. Some persons smoke 100-millimeter cigarettes. International airline passengers may be informed of the limit to the weight of their luggage in both pounds and kilograms.

Some units in the metric system are the same as those in our customary system. The second, for example, is a unit of time in the metric system. If you have any interest in electricity, you probably are familiar with the ampere, a unit of electric current in both systems. Perhaps only those persons who have studied light know that the candela, a unit of luminous intensity, is the same in both systems.

The metric system that France adopted in 1799 has been changed a little since then, and it probably will continue to be changed somewhat. In 1875 several nations formed the General Conference on Weights and Measures, which promotes the adoption of standard units of weights and measures by all countries of the world. From time to time, it redefines units or creates new ones as the need arises. In 1960, one of its committees, the International Committee on Weights and Measures, adopted a modern version of the metric system called *Système International d'Unités,* or, in English, International System of Units. Its abbreviation is SI in all countries no matter what language is spoken. Undoubtedly we will continue to call it the metric system for many years to come, but you should know both names.

The rules of SI are few. For each quantity to be measured there is only one unit, but from that unit we may derive a number of multiples and submultiples as explained later in this chapter. There are seven base units, two supplementary units, and several derived units. Most of these are of interest only to scientists or certain craftsmen or professional persons, and we will discuss in this book only those likely to be used by the average person. However, a table in the Appendix lists all of them, so that you can refer to any that might be of special interest to you.

The seven base units are the meter (for length), the kilogram (strictly speaking, for mass, but applied to weight in everyday terms), the kelvin (for temperature), the second (for time), the ampere (for electric current), the candela (for luminous intensity), and the mole (for amount of substance).

The Appendix also gives the definition of each unit. Unless you are an expert in physics, you probably won't understand most of them. The meter, for example, is defined as a multiple of the wavelength of light of one particular color. Most persons would not have the slightest idea of how to determine that wavelength, and of the few that do, many don't have the equipment with which to do it. Then why are such definitions used? Because they are quite precise. Much of the machinery we use in our modern world is made of parts that must fit together exactly. An error in size equal to the thickness of one of your hairs—or just a fraction of that thickness—can make some equipment useless. You cannot get that kind of accuracy with barleycorns or a copy of a stick once held along King Edgar's arm.

Another advantage of the metric system is that its base units can be checked at any time by those who have the proper equipment. Such persons can check the exact length of a meter whenever it is necessary, but we cannot go back in time to measure King Edgar again. If you had 36 barleycorns to put end to end, they wouldn't be exactly the same length as a set of 36 barleycorns used to determine the length of a foot a thousand years ago. The wavelength of light of a particular color does not change, and therefore we can rely on it to be an accurate measure with which to determine the length of the meter. The standards for other units of the metric system have been chosen similarly for their reproducibility, if not for their immediate convenience. Of course, the average person will not be checking the precise length of a meter. He will use his meterstick just as he uses his yardstick now.

Each base unit of the metric system has its own symbol. They are listed in Table 1. Unlike some abbreviations, the symbols are not followed by periods. Their singular and plural forms are the same. Thus, 1 m indi-

## TABLE 1

### SI Base Units

| QUANTITY | UNIT | SI SYMBOL |
|---|---|---|
| length | meter | m |
| weight (mass) | kilogram | kg |
| time | second | s |
| electric current | ampere | A |
| thermodynamic temperature | kelvin | K |
| luminous intensity | candela | cd |
| amount of substance | mole | mol |

cates one meter; 2 m, not 2 ms, indicates two meters.

Symbols are not capitalized unless the name of the unit was taken from the name of a person, such as André Marie Ampère, who discovered some of the principles of electricity. The name of the unit is never capitalized. So A stands for ampere.

For each base unit in the metric system (and for each supplementary and each derived unit, too) there is a series of units that are multiples or submultiples of that unit. For instance, the prefix deka multiplies a unit by 10; a dekameter equals 10 meters. The prefix hecto multiplies a unit by 100; a hectosecond equals 100 seconds. The prefix deci divides a unit by 10; a decimeter is 0.1 meters. The prefix centi divides a unit by 100; a centimeter equals 0.01 meters. These and other prefixes for larger multiples and smaller submultiples are given in Table 2. The case of the kilogram is an exception to this way of naming multiples and submultiples of base units, and that is explained in Chapter 5.

TABLE 2

SI Prefixes

| PREFIX | SYMBOL | MULTIPLICATION FACTOR | MULTIPLICATION FACTOR IN EXPONENTIAL FORM |
|---|---|---|---|
| tera | T | 1,000,000,000,000 | $10^{12}$ |
| giga | G | 1,000,000,000 | $10^{9}$ |
| mega | M | 1,000,000 | $10^{6}$ |
| kilo | k | 1,000 | $10^{3}$ |
| hecto | h | 100 | $10^{2}$ |
| deka | da | 10 | $10^{1}$ |
| deci | d | 0.1 | $10^{-1}$ |
| centi | c | 0.01 | $10^{-2}$ |
| milli | m | 0.001 | $10^{-3}$ |
| micro | $\mu$ | 0.000,001 | $10^{-6}$ |
| nano[1] | n | 0.000,000,001 | $10^{-9}$ |
| pico[2] | p | 0.000,000,000,001 | $10^{-12}$ |
| femto | f | 0.000,000,000,000,001 | $10^{-15}$ |
| atto | a | 0.000,000,000,000,000,001 | $10^{-18}$ |

[1] Formerly millimicro (m$\mu$)
[2] Formerly micromicro ($\mu\mu$)

Once you know the names of the base units that interest you and the names of the most used prefixes, you can put them together to form any unit that you are likely to use. If you understand, for instance, that there are a thousand millimeters in a meter, then you will know that there are a thousand milliseconds in a second, and a thousand milligrams in a gram. For most everyday purposes, you probably will not use prefixes larger than kilo (1,000 times) or possibly mega

(1,000,000 times) or smaller than milli (0.001, or one thousandth) or possibly micro (0.000,001, or one millionth), so there really isn't very much to learn.

The prefixes enable us to avoid using very small or very large numbers if we don't want to be bothered with them. We can express sizes of many things in numbers no smaller than 1 and no larger than 1,000 just by choosing the appropriate prefix. This line ___ is 0.003 meter long, but you might prefer to say that it is 3 millimeters long, which is the same thing. This line ______________ is 0.03 meter long, but you could also say it is 30 millimeters (or 3 centimeters) long. If you were a biologist studying viruses, you probably would say that an influenza virus has a diameter of about 100 nanometers rather than 0.000,000,1 meter. An airline pilot prefers to say that the air distance from London to Paris is 343 kilometers rather than 343,000 meters. He also prefers to say that the air distance from London to Sydney, Australia is approximately 17,000 kilometers rather than 17,000,000 meters. He could, of

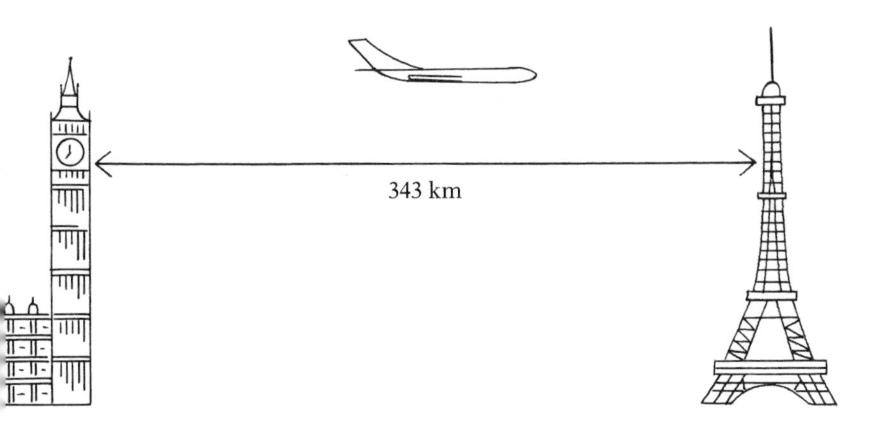

course, express that distance as 17 megameters, but ordinarily he would prefer the larger number in order to express all distances in the same units—kilometers, in this case.

To convert from one unit to another unit all you have to do is to move the decimal point the correct number of places. For instance, if you want to convert a meter to millimeters, you merely move the decimal point three places to the right. Just write one meter as 1.0 with as many more zeros after it as necessary.[1] Then move the decimal point:

1.0000 meters = 1,000.0 millimeters

How many millimeters are there in 5 kilometers? Because there are 1,000,000 millimeters in a kilometer, you must move the decimal point six places to the right:

5.0000000 kilometers = 5,000,000.0 millimeters

Let's reverse these two problems. How many meters in a millimeter? Take 1 millimeter and move the decimal point three places to the left (add zeros to the left of the number whenever necessary):

0001.0 millimeter = 0.001 meter

How many kilometers in a millimeter? Take 1 millimeter and move the decimal point six places to the left:

0000001.0 millimeter = 0.000,001 kilometer

1. Adding zeros after a number with a decimal point in it does not change its value; 1 = 1.0 = 1.00 = 1.000, and so on. Just be sure you don't put a zero between a decimal point and a digit; 0.1 does not equal 0.01, nor does 1.0 equal 10.0.

Is there a quick method for determining how many places you must move a decimal point to make a conversion from one unit to another? Yes. Look at the last column in Table 2. In this column the multiplication factor of each prefix is expressed in exponential form.[2] The exponent in each case is the superscript—the small number written above the line. Suppose you want to determine how many kilometers there are in a gigameter. The exponent of the multiplication factor for kilometers is 3 and that for gigameters is 9. Subtract 3 from 9, and the answer is 6. So you move the decimal point six places to the right:

1.0000000 gigameter = 1,000,000.0 kilometers

If you wanted to make the conversion in the other direction, from kilometers to gigameters, then you would subtract 9 from 3 and get the answer −6. You would then move the decimal point six places to the left:

0000001.0 kilometer = 0.000,001 gigameter

Always begin with the exponent corresponding to the unit you want to convert from and subtract from it the exponent corresponding to the unit you want to convert to. The resulting number tells you how many places to move the decimal point. If the number is positive, move the decimal point to the right; if the number is negative, move the decimal point to the left.

You might find it convenient to remember the following rules for placing the decimal point.

2. If you are not familiar with exponents, you can read about them in the Appendix, but you don't really have to understand them to be able to perform the conversions described here.

To multiply or divide by 10, move the decimal point one place.

To multiply or divide by 100, move the decimal point two places.

To multiply or divide by 1,000, move the decimal point three places.

To multiply (by a whole number), move the decimal place to the right.

To divide (by a whole number), move the decimal place to the left.

Each prefix has its own symbol. All but one of them are letters with which you are familiar. The symbol for micro is $\mu$, the Greek letter mu, which corresponds to our letter *m*. The symbol for a prefix is placed directly before the symbol for a base unit. The symbol for a centimeter is cm, for a millisecond ms, for a kilometer km, and so on.

No unit may have more than one prefix. Thus a kilometer (1,000 meters) is never called a dekahectometer (which would mean $10 \times 100$ meters, which equals 1,000 meters, too). Before the adoption of the SI version of the metric system, the prefixes millimicro and micromicro were used. Now they are replaced by nano and pico, respectively. You may still see these obsolete double prefixes in old books, however.

Because the multiples and submultiples of each SI unit are related to each other by factors of 10, 100, 1,000, and so forth, once people have gone to the small trouble of learning the metric system (which is much easier to learn than our customary system) they will find that many everyday arithmetic problems can be solved much faster than they are now. Business firms will save money because employees will need less time to solve problems, and schoolchildren will be able to learn the units of measurement in less time, and they probably will remember them longer. Did you ever learn how many pecks there are in a bushel? If so, do you remember it now, or do you have to look it up?

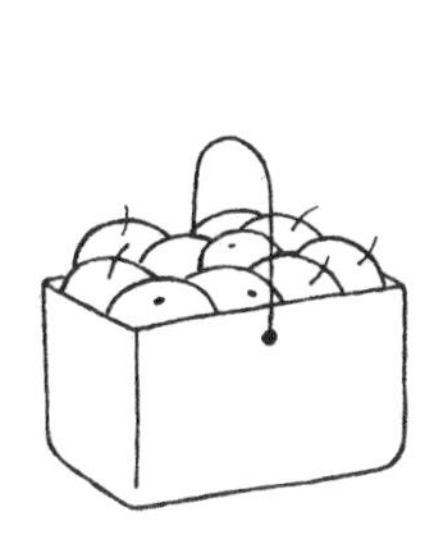

# 2 *Length and the Metric System*

When France adopted the Metric System in 1799, it was decided that all metric units would be derived from some unchanging aspect of the natural world. So the meter (also spelled metre) was to be based on the distance between the North Pole and the Equator. Surveyors were employed to survey a straight line that extended from the North Pole to a point near Paris and continued on to the Equator. It took several years to finish the work, and when it was done, the meter was declared to be one ten-millionth ($^1/_{10,000,000}$) of the length of that line. Until recently, the meter was defined this way.

Theoretically, anyone who wanted to check the length of a meter could survey the same line, but, of course, that would be very expensive and time-consuming. Therefore, a platinum bar was made, and two marks exactly one meter apart were cut into the bar. This bar was kept by the French government to serve as the international standard of the meter. Later, France made several copies of this bar and presented them to nations that were members of the General Conference of Weights and Measures. The United States has two copies made from an alloy of platinum and iridium; this alloy is more durable than platinum alone.

You probably think of a metal bar as something that ordinarily does not change. However, metal does contract and expand with changes in temperature, and

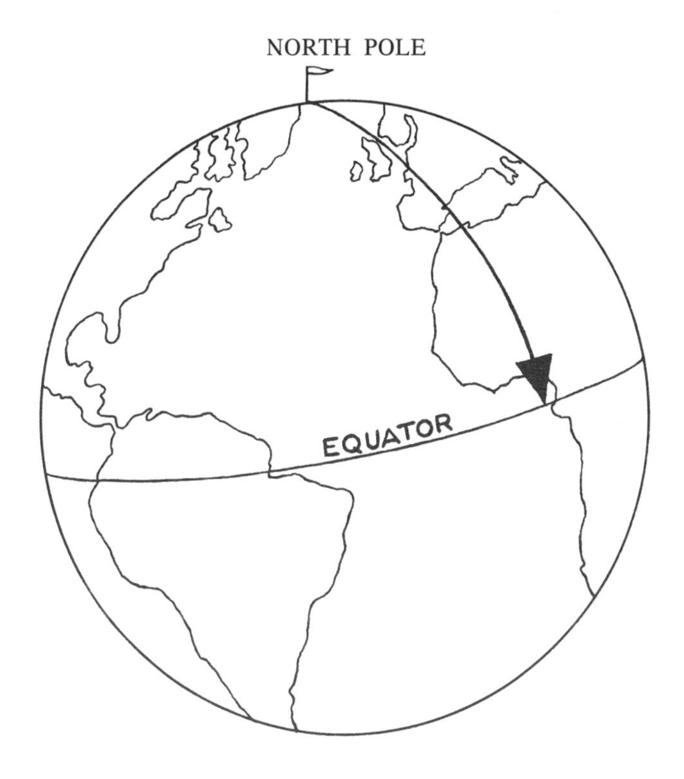

these meter bars had to be protected as much as possible from temperature changes. Most countries keep theirs in air conditioned cases where the bars cannot be touched by dust or polluting gases in the atmosphere nor subjected to temperature changes. Even so, the bars probably change slightly in length—not enough that most persons would ever notice it, but enough to make them inaccurate for extremely precise measurements. Then, too, a metal bar carefully kept in a sealed case cannot be used by just anyone. Only a few persons could be allowed to examine it. Like King Edgar's arm, it could be made directly available to only a few persons.

To make matters worse—or perhaps just annoying—it was discovered that the original determination of the distance between the North Pole and the Equator was in error. The error was extremely small, but it meant that the meter really didn't have a natural base.

Today the meter is precisely defined in terms of the wavelength of orange-red light emitted by a krypton atom undergoing a particular change in energy content; the meter is defined as a multiple of the wavelength of this light (see Appendix). Although the average person cannot determine this wavelength, many laboratories all over the world are equipped to do so.

The average person, of course, is not interested in such precision. How big is a meter in everyday terms? An American probably will understand it better when told that a meter is a little longer than a yard—39.37 inches. A meter is too long to draw on this page, but this line is one decimeter long. A meter, then, is ten times longer.

A centimeter is this long: _____ If you have a ruler marked in both centimeters and inches, you may have noticed that 30 centimeters nearly equal a foot.

A millimeter is this long: _ A dot 0.1 millimeter in diameter is the smallest thing most persons can see without the aid of a magnifying glass or microscope. Of course, people vary in their ability to see, so some

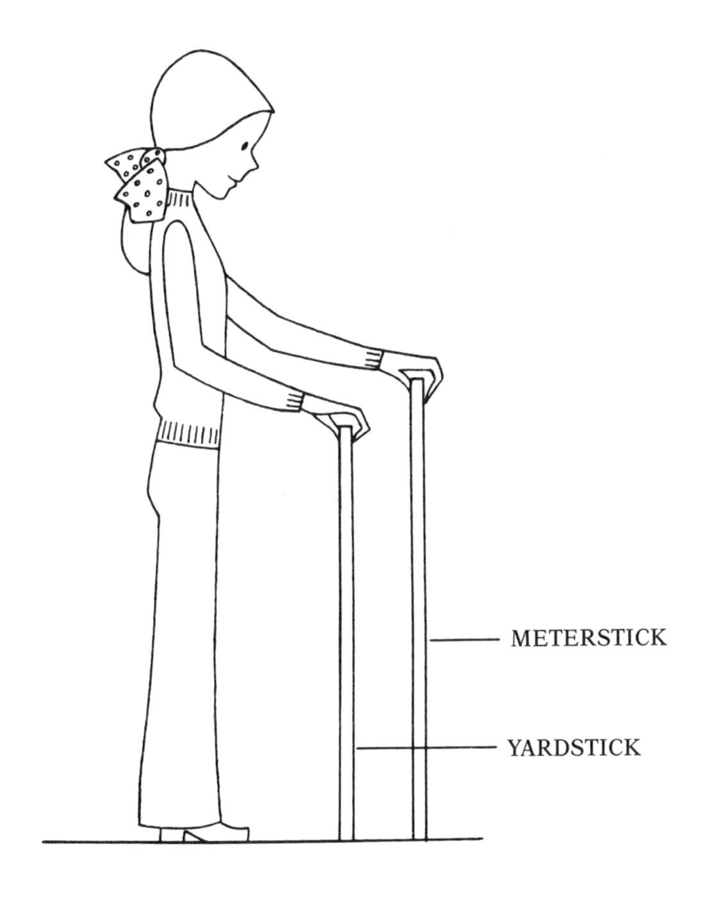

persons might not be able to see anything that small, but others might see objects slightly smaller.

To become familiar with meters, decimeters, centimeters, and millimeters you might get a meterstick and a metric ruler and practice measuring some familiar things near you. How tall is your kitchen table? How long? How wide? What is the diameter of a penny? A dime? A nickel? A quarter? How long and how wide is a dollar bill? A postage stamp? How long is an inch? A foot? A yard? Measure your room or some of the windows in your house. How tall are you?

Objects less than about 0.1 millimeter in size can be viewed only with the aid of a magnifying glass or a microscope. Some of the microscopes that you might use in a biology class at school are used for examining objects that have diameters ranging from about 1 micrometer to 100 micrometers. (Can you convert 100 micrometers to millimeters? Does your answer correspond with anything mentioned above?)

Before the adoption of the SI version of the metric system, a micrometer was called a micron (abbreviated $\mu$), and many persons still call it that today. Books published in the 1960s or earlier use the term *micron,* but most books published more recently use *micrometer.*

You should become familiar with units larger than a meter, too. With a meterstick, lay off 10 meters, and you will have measured a dekameter. Unless your home or school has very large rooms, you might have to do this in a hall, in a basement, or outdoors.

Measuring off a kilometer will require a little more trouble. You could mark the length of one dekameter on a piece of twine and then take the twine outdoors

TABLE 3

Some Conversions of Units of Length
in the Metric System

| KILOMETERS (km) | | METERS (m) | | DECIMETERS (dm) | | CENTIMETERS (cm) | | MILLIMETERS (mm) |
|---|---|---|---|---|---|---|---|---|
| 1 km | = | 1,000 m | = | 10,000 dm | = | 100,000 cm | = | 1,000,000 mm |
| 0.001 km | = | 1 m | = | 10 dm | = | 100 cm | = | 1,000 mm |
| 0.000,1 km | = | 0.1 m | = | 1 dm | = | 10 cm | = | 100 mm |
| 0.000,01 km | = | 0.01 m | = | 0.1 dm | = | 1 cm | = | 10 mm |
| 0.000,001 km | = | 0.001 m | = | 0.01 dm | = | 0.1 cm | = | 1 mm |

TABLE 4

Some Conversions of Units of Length
in the Customary System

| MILES (mi) | | YARDS (yd) | | FEET (ft) | | INCHES (in) |
|---|---|---|---|---|---|---|
| 1 mi | = | 1,760 yd | = | 5,280 ft | = | 63,360 in |
| $\frac{1}{1,760}$ mi | = | 1 yd | = | 3 ft | = | 36 in |
| $\frac{1}{5,280}$ mi | = | $\frac{1}{3}$ yd | = | 1 ft | = | 12 in |
| $\frac{1}{63,360}$ mi | = | $\frac{1}{36}$ yd | = | $\frac{1}{12}$ ft | = | 1 in |

and measure off 100 dekameters. It might be easier to do this if you take a friend along to help you. To avoid the danger of working in a street, you might measure your kilometer on the sidewalk and just continue your way around the block whenever you come to corners. Perhaps a kilometer will take you around the block more than once.

What is the distance around your school? One lap around the gym? Or one lap around the football field or track if your school has one? How long does it take you to walk a kilometer? Can you estimate the distance from your home to your school? If the distance is so long that you have to go by bus or automobile, watch the odometer and record the distance in miles. Then multiply the number of miles by 1.6 to get the number of kilometers. You can measure off one kilometer by watching the odometer for 0.6 mile.

Table 3 summarizes conversions between some of the

most commonly used units of length in the metric system. Of course, you really don't need this table, for as long as you know what each of the prefixes means you should be able to convert any metric unit of length into another quickly. Perhaps by now you have learned some of them without even trying. Table 3 is there so that you can compare it with conversions between some of the most commonly used units of length in our customary system, which are summarized in Table 4. Notice how much more clumsy the customary system is.

Let's look at an example of a simple arithmetic problem in each system. Suppose you had a board 50 inches long and wanted to cut it into three boards of equal length. You would divide 50 by 3 to determine the length of each new board. The answer is $16\frac{2}{3}$ inches. It's easy enough to find 16 inches and 17 inches on a yardstick, but inches are not divided into thirds on our yardsticks–they are divided into halves, fourths, eighths, and sometimes sixteenths. How do you find two-thirds of an inch? The best thing to do is to choose the finest division your yardstick has–say eighths. One inch equals $\frac{8}{8}$ inch. Two-thirds of 8 is $5\frac{1}{3}$. Therefore, two-thirds of $\frac{8}{8}$ is $\frac{5\frac{1}{3}}{8}$, or somewhere between $\frac{5}{8}$ and $\frac{6}{8}$. So the spot you are looking for on your yardstick is between $16\frac{5}{8}$ and $16\frac{6}{8}$. This particular problem involves the performing of two separate steps: first the inches are divided by 3, and when the answer turns out to contain a fraction, that fraction has to be converted to eighths of an inch.

Now look at a similar problem in the metric system.

You have a board 50 centimeters long and want to cut it into three equal pieces. Once you notice that 3 does not go into 50 a whole number of times, you can convert the 50 centimeters into the finest divisions on your meterstick—probably millimeters. By now you might be able to perform that conversion in your head:

$$50 \text{ centimeters} = 500 \text{ millimeters}$$

Now divide 500 millimeters by 3:

$$\begin{array}{r} 166\tfrac{2}{3} \text{ millimeters} \\ 3\overline{)500} \end{array}$$

You will find the correct spot on your meterstick between 166 and 167 millimeters (or between 16.6 centimeters and 16.7 centimeters if you prefer to convert back to centimeters, but there is no reason why that should be necessary).

Although the second problem really requires the performing of two separate steps, one of them—multiplication by 10 to convert centimeters into millimeters—is so easy that you can hardly consider it any work at all. So for all practical purposes we can consider the problem solved by performing only one moderately "difficult" step—division by 3.

On almost every road map there is in one corner a legend that includes a line that is divided into units —miles in the United States and kilometers in metric countries. This line tells you that distance on the map represents so many miles or so many kilometers. Maps in metric countries often have a notation something like this "Scale 1:1,000,000." This means that distances in the real world are 1,000,000 times what they are on the map. To put it another way, it means that one centimeter on the map stands for 1,000,000 centimeters on land or sea. Of course, no one wants to measure distances between cities in centimeters; we would prefer to think in terms of kilometers. So, how many kilometers are there in 1,000,000 centimeters? Move the decimal point five places to the left (review Chapter 1 if you don't understand why). The answer is 10 kilometers. Therefore, one centimeter on the map stands for 10 kilometers. If the distance between two cities on the map is 2.5 centimeters, you know that the real distance between the cities is 25 kilometers.

Other maps, of course, may have different scales. If the scale is 1:625,000, then take 625,000 and move the decimal point five places to the left. On such a map, one centimeter stands for 6.25 kilometers.

If the legend of an American map were to tell you the scale was 1:1,000,000, to determine how many miles an inch stands for you would have to divide 1,000,000 by the number of inches in a mile: 63,360. No wonder American maps rarely give you the scale that way.

If you had a map of just your neighborhood or the blueprint of a building, you might want to know how many meters a centimeter stands for. Can you determine how many meters a centimeter stands for if the scale is 1:1,000? If it is 1:100?

# 3 Area and the Metric System

There is no need for a special unit of area in the metric system, for all measurements of area can be expressed by using derived units: the square meter and its multiples and submultiples. A square with each edge one meter long has an area of one square meter, a square with each edge one centimeter long has an area of one square centimeter, and so on. Of course, areas with other shapes can have an area of one square meter or one square centimeter. For instance, a rectangle 2 meters long and a half meter wide has an area of one square meter. The area of any plane figure is calculated the same way it is when you use the customary system, but, of course, you use metric units instead.

1 m × 1 m = 1 m²
2 m × ½ m = 1 m²

The symbols for units of area include the numeral *2* written as a superscript. A square meter is indicated by the symbol $m^2$, a square kilometer by $km^2$, a square millimeter by $mm^2$, and so on.

You must be sure that you don't confuse the superscript 2 used to indicate a square unit and the superscript 2 used to indicate a number squared. For instance:

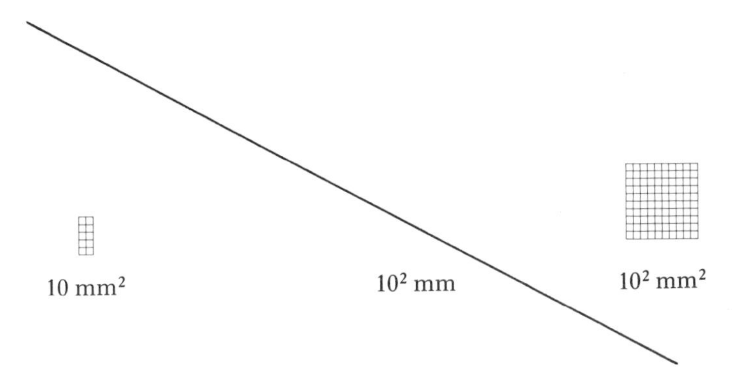


$10\ mm^2$ means ten square millimeters. This is a measurement of area.

$10^2\ mm$ means one hundred (or ten squared, which is $10 \times 10$) millimeters. This is a measurement of length.

$10^2\ mm^2$ means one hundred square millimeters. This is a measurement of area.

To become familiar with metric units of area you might calculate the areas of a few things by using convenient metric units of length. An ordinary postage stamp is 22 mm wide and 25 mm tall. Its area is 22 mm $\times$ 25 mm or 550 mm$^2$. What is the area of a dollar bill? Of the cover of this book? The notebook paper you ordinarily use? The floor of your room?

The conversion factors for units of area are not the same as those for units of length. A centimeter is ten times as long as a millimeter, but a square centimeter is one hundred times as large as a square millimeter. If a square is one centimeter long on each edge, then we can say that it is 10 millimeters long on each edge. If we calculate the area using centimeters, we express the area as

$$1 \text{ cm} \times 1 \text{ cm} = 1 \text{ cm}^2$$

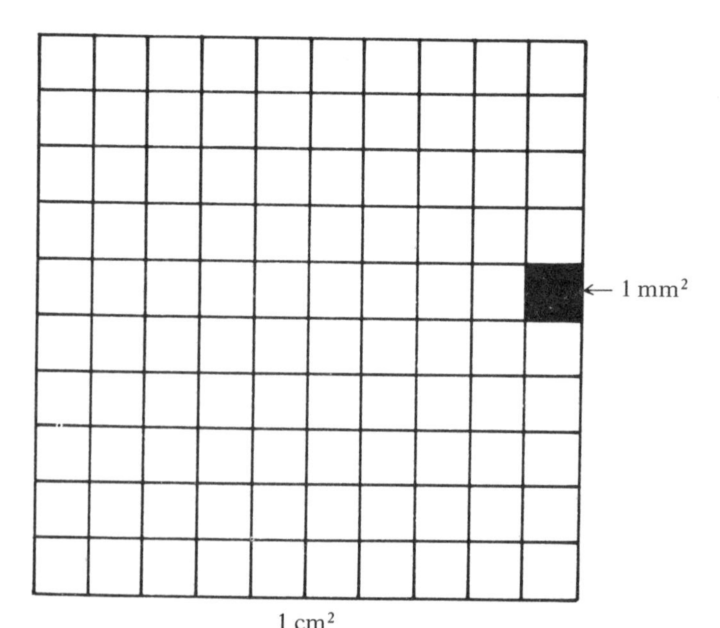


1 cm$^2$

If we calculate the area using millimeters, we express the area as

$$10 \text{ mm} \times 10 \text{ mm} = 100 \text{ mm}^2 \text{ (or } 10^2 \text{ mm}^2\text{)}$$

If the postage stamp mentioned above had been measured in centimeters, we would say that it is 2.2 cm wide and 2.5 cm tall. Its area is 2.2 cm $\times$ 2.5 cm, or 5.50 $\text{cm}^2$.

There are 1,000 millimeters in a meter. How many square millimeters are there in a square meter? Multiply 1,000 mm $\times$ 1,000 mm, and the answer is 1,000,000 $\text{mm}^2$ (or $10^6$ $\text{mm}^2$).

Table 5 summarizes some conversion factors of area in the metric system. Some of the numbers are very large and others are very small, but conversions in the metric system still are more convenient to work with than are the conversion factors for area in the customary system, a few of which are given in Table 6.

## TABLE 5

Some Conversions of Units of Area
in the Metric System

| SQUARE KILOMETERS ($km^2$) | | SQUARE METERS ($m^2$) | | SQUARE DECIMETERS ($dm^2$) | | SQUARE CENTIMETERS ($cm^2$) | | SQUARE MILLIMET ($mm^2$) |
|---|---|---|---|---|---|---|---|---|
| 1 $km^2$ | = | 1,000,000 $m^2$ | | | | | | |
| 0.000,001 $km^2$ | = | 1 $m^2$ | = | 100 $dm^2$ | = | 10,000 $cm^2$ | = | 1,000,000 r |
| | | 0.01 $m^2$ | = | 1 $dm^2$ | = | 100 $cm^2$ | = | 10,000 m |
| | | 0.000,1 $m^2$ | = | 0.01 $dm^2$ | = | 1 $cm^2$ | = | 100 mm |
| | | 0.000,001 $m^2$ | = | 0.000,1 $dm^2$ | = | 0.01 $cm^2$ | = | 1 mm |

## TABLE 6

Some Conversions of Units of Area
in the Customary System

| SQUARE MILES (sq mi) | | ACRES | | SQUARE YARDS (sq yd) | | SQUARE FEET (sq ft) | | SQUARE IN (sq in) |
|---|---|---|---|---|---|---|---|---|
| 1 sq mi | = | 640 acres | | | | | | |
| $\frac{1}{640}$ sq mi | = | 1 acre | = | 4,840 sq yd | | | | |
| | | $\frac{1}{4,840}$ acre | = | 1 sq yd | = | 9 sq ft | | |
| | | | | $\frac{1}{9}$ sq yd | = | 1 sq ft | = | 144 sq |
| | | | | | | $\frac{1}{144}$ sq ft | = | 1 sq in |

# 4 *Volume and the Metric System*

There is no need for a base unit of volume in the metric system, for, like area, volume can be expressed by using derived units: the cubic meter and its multiples and submultiples. A cube with each edge one meter long has a volume of one cubic meter, a cube with each edge one centimeter long has a volume of one cubic centimeter, and so on.

The symbols for the units of volume include the numeral *3* written as a superscript. For instance, a cubic meter is indicated by the symbol $m^3$, a cubic kilometer by $km^3$, a cubic millimeter by $mm^3$, and so on. In some older books you may find the cubic centimeter ($cm^3$) abbreviated as cu. cm. or c.c. or cc. In fact, when speaking, scientists still often call it a c.c. (pronounced see-see).

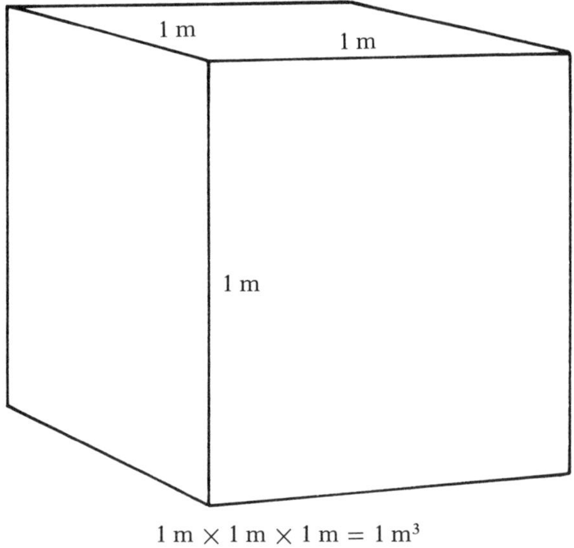


$1 \text{ m} \times 1 \text{ m} \times 1 \text{ m} = 1 \text{ m}^3$

You must be sure that you don't confuse the superscript 3 used to indicate a cubic unit and the superscript 3 used to indicate a number cubed. For instance:

$10 \text{ mm}^3$ means ten cubic millimeters. This is a measurement of volume.

$10^3$ mm means one thousand (or ten cubed, which

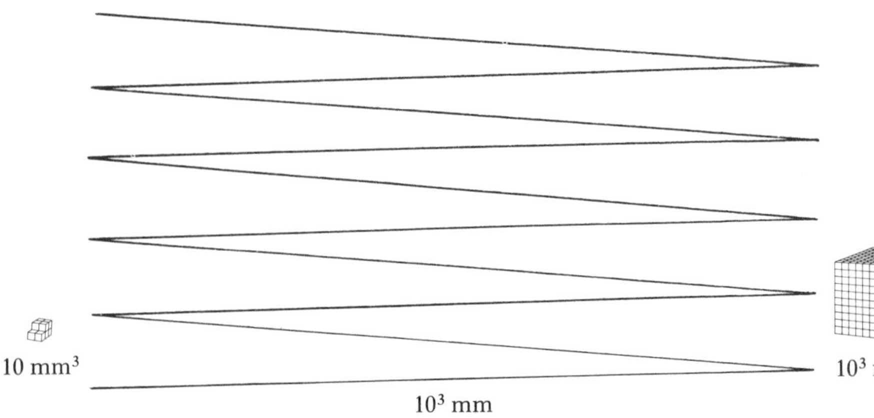

equals $10 \times 10 \times 10$) millimeters. This is a measurement of length.

$10^3$ mm$^3$ means one thousand cubic millimeters. This is a measurement of volume.

To become familiar with metric units of volume you might calculate the volumes of several things. To make your calculations easy, use only objects of fairly regular shape with straight edges, such as some boxes, a brick, or a room.

After performing only a few calculations you will notice that you are working with some surprisingly large numbers. A cube that is one centimeter on an edge has a volume of 1 cubic centimeter, but if you convert these measurements to millimeters, you will find that the same cube has a volume of 1,000 cubic millimeters:

$$10 \text{ mm} \times 10 \text{ mm} \times 10 \text{ mm} = 1{,}000 \text{ mm}^3$$

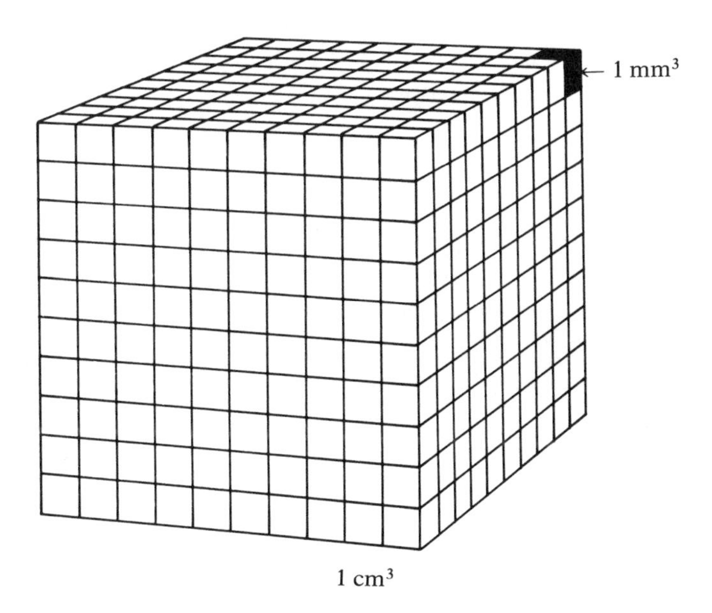

Despite the fact that we have no need for special units of volume in the metric system, the original metric system did have them: the liter (also spelled litre) and its multiples and submultiples. The liter is equal to a cubic decimeter.

The liter has become so popular in metric countries that, despite the fact that we don't need it, it continues to be used in those countries, and when the United States adopts the metric system, we almost certainly will ask to purchase milk, gasoline, and other liquids in liters and not in cubic decimeters. The SI version of the metric system does not recognize the liter as an official unit of measurement, but gives it a special status as an "allowed" unit.

The symbol for a liter is l. Prefixes like kilo and milli are applied to multiples and submultiples of the liter just as they are in the case of official SI units. The symbol for kiloliter is kl, for milliliter is ml, and so on.

If you want to see how large a liter is, cut five squares from cardboard. Each square should be one decimeter long on each edge. Tape the five squares together to

## TABLE 7

Some Conversions of Units of Volume in the Metric System

| CUBIC KILOMETERS ($km^3$) | | CUBIC METERS ($m^3$) | | CUBIC DECIMETERS ($dm^3$) | | CUBIC CENTIMETERS ($cm^3$) | | CUBIC MILLIMETERS ($mm^3$) |
|---|---|---|---|---|---|---|---|---|
| 1 $km^3$ | = | 1,000,000,000 $m^3$ | | | | | | |
| 0.000,000,001 $km^3$ | = | 1 $m^3$ (1 kiloliter) | = | 1,000 $dm^3$ | = | 1,000,000 $cm^3$ | = | 1,000,000,000 $mm^3$ |
| | | 0.001 $m^3$ | = | 1 $dm^3$ (1 liter) | = | 1,000 $cm^3$ | = | 1,000,000 $mm^3$ |
| | | 0.000,001 $m^3$ | = | 0.001 $dm^3$ | = | 1 $cm^3$ (1 milliliter) | = | 1,000 $mm^3$ |
| | | 0.000,000,001 $m^3$ | = | 0.000,001 $dm^3$ | = | 0.001 $cm^3$ | = | 1 $mm^3$ |

## TABLE 8

### Some Conversions of Units of Volume in the Customary System

| CUBIC MILES (cu mi) | | CUBIC YARDS (cu yd) | | CUBIC FEET (cu ft) | | CUBIC INCHES (cu in) |
|---|---|---|---|---|---|---|
| 1 cu mi | = | 5,451,776,000 cu yd | | | | |
| $\frac{1}{5,451,776,000}$ cu mi | = | 1 cu yd | = | 27 cu ft | | |
| | | $\frac{1}{27}$ cu yd | = | 1 cu ft | = | 1,728 cu in |
| | | | | $\frac{1}{1,728}$ cu ft | = | 1 cu in |

## TABLE 9

### Some Additional Conversions of Units of Volume in the Customary System

DRY CAPACITY

| BUSHELS (bu) | | PECKS (pk) | | QUARTS (qt) | | PINTS (pt) |
|---|---|---|---|---|---|---|
| 1 bu | = | 4 pk | = | 8 qt | = | 16 pt |
| $\frac{1}{4}$ bu | = | 1 pk | = | 2 qt | = | 4 pt |
| $\frac{1}{8}$ bu | = | $\frac{1}{2}$ pk | = | 1 qt | = | 2 pt |
| $\frac{1}{16}$ bu | = | $\frac{1}{4}$ pk | = | $\frac{1}{2}$ qt | = | 1 pt |

TABLE 9 (continued)

LIQUID CAPACITY

| GALLONS (gal) | | QUARTS (qt) | | PINTS (pt) | | CUPS (c) | | FLUIDOUNCES (fl oz) | | TABLESPOONS (tbs) | | TEASPOONS (tsp) |
|---|---|---|---|---|---|---|---|---|---|---|---|---|
| 1 gal | = | 4 qt | = | 8 pt | = | 16 c | = | 128 fl oz | = | 256 tbs | = | 768 tsp |
| $\frac{1}{4}$ gal | = | 1 qt | = | 2 pt | = | 4 c | = | 32 fl oz | = | 64 tbs | = | 192 tsp |
| $\frac{1}{8}$ gal | = | $\frac{1}{2}$ qt | = | 1 pt | = | 2 c | = | 16 fl oz | = | 32 tbs | = | 96 tsp |
| $\frac{1}{16}$ gal | = | $\frac{1}{4}$ qt | = | $\frac{1}{2}$ pt | = | 1 c | = | 8 fl oz | = | 16 tbs | = | 48 tsp |
| $\frac{1}{128}$ gal | = | $\frac{1}{32}$ qt | = | $\frac{1}{16}$ pt | = | $\frac{1}{8}$ c | = | 1 fl oz | = | 2 tbs | = | 6 tsp |
| $\frac{1}{256}$ gal | = | $\frac{1}{64}$ qt | = | $\frac{1}{32}$ pt | = | $\frac{1}{16}$ c | = | $\frac{1}{2}$ fl oz | = | 1 tbs | = | 3 tsp |
| $\frac{1}{768}$ gal | = | $\frac{1}{192}$ qt | = | $\frac{1}{96}$ pt | = | $\frac{1}{48}$ c | = | $\frac{1}{6}$ fl oz | = | $\frac{1}{3}$ tbs | = | 1 tsp |

form a box open at the top. This box holds one liter. This is a little more than a quart (a liquid quart in the United States, that is—the U.S. dry quart is a little larger than a liter, and a British liquid quart is a little larger than a U.S. dry quart).

You can easily make another box that holds one milliliter. Just cut five squares one centimeter on an edge and tape them together the same way. Five milliliters are nearly equal to a teaspoon, and 15 milliliters are nearly equal to a tablespoon.

Table 7 summarizes some conversion factors of volume in the metric system. Note that:

1 kiloliter = 1 cubic meter
1 liter = 1 cubic decimeter
1 milliliter = 1 cubic centimeter

Notice also, that when you use the liter as a unit of volume, you don't have to say that it is cubed, because the word liter is used only for volume and never for length or area.

Table 8 contains a few conversion factors of volume in the customary system. In addition to expressing volume in terms of cubic inches, cubic feet, and so on, the customary system has special units for both liquids and dry material; some of these units are included in Table 9. A comparison of Table 7 with Tables 8 and 9 shows the metric system to be simpler once again.

If you're still not convinced, let's examine one small problem in volume that a cook might face. An American cook must remember that there are three teaspoons in a tablespoon. A set of American measuring spoons usually consists of four spoons: a tablespoon,

a teaspoon, a half-teaspoon, and a quarter-teaspoon. Suppose a recipe calls for $1\frac{1}{2}$ tablespoons of salt. How do you measure out $1\frac{1}{2}$ tablespoons of something? You can use the tablespoon to get one tablespoon of salt, but there is no measuring spoon for a half-tablespoon. Now you must convert to teaspoons. If there are three teaspoons in one tablespoon, then

$$\frac{1}{2} \text{ tablespoon} = 1\frac{1}{2} \text{ teaspoons}$$

So to get the remaining half-tablespoon you must measure out one teaspoonful and one half-teaspoonful.

A recipe in the metric system would call for a certain number of milliliters of salt—perhaps 20 or 25 ml. Of course, you might have to use more than one spoon or the same spoon twice, but you would not have to convert to any other unit. You would just measure out in milliliters whatever the recipe calls for in milliliters.

Because the United States has not adopted the metric system, we do not know yet what size our metric spoons will be. Some persons would like a set of metric spoons to include a 5-ml spoon and a 15-ml spoon because these correspond closely to a teaspoon and a tablespoon, respectively. Using them, you could get 20 ml of salt by filling the 15-ml spoon once and the 5-ml spoon once. You could get 25 ml of salt by filling the 15-ml spoon once and the 5-ml spoon twice. Of course, we may have a different combination of metric spoons, but whatever they turn out to be, they probably will be easier to use than our present measuring spoons.

If you have the time, work out this problem: your recipe calls for $1\frac{1}{2}$ tablespoons of salt, but you are going to make only half the recipe, so you will need only $\frac{3}{4}$ tablespoon of salt. How do you measure it out? How much easier it is to take half of 20 ml (or even 25 ml) of salt.

# 5 Weight and the Metric System

The base unit for measuring weight (actually for measuring mass[3]) is the kilogram (also spelled kilogramme). Why the kilogram and not the gram? In the original version of the metric system, the gram was a base unit, and it was defined as the weight (mass) of one cubic centimeter of water at the melting point of ice. A cubic centimeter is a rather small quantity, and it is difficult to check its weight accurately. Therefore, SI uses a quantity a thousand times larger, a kilogram, as the base unit.

Today the standard for the kilogram is a cylinder of a specific size of an alloy of platinum and iridium. It is kept by the International Bureau of Weights and

3. An explanation of the difference between mass and weight may be found on page 79.

Measures in Paris. Many countries, including the United States, have copies of this cylinder.

Because the term kilogram already possesses a prefix, it was decided that the prefixes for its multiples and submultiples would be determined as if the gram were the base unit. Otherwise we would have to put up with some ridiculous units like millikilogram ($^{1}/_{1,000}$ of 1,000 grams) when we actually mean what by long custom we have called a gram—and still do. Another possibility, of course, was to give a completely new name to the kilogram, but because the gram and its multiples and submultiples were such familiar units in metric countries, it was decided not to take this choice. So familiar is the kilogram that it sometimes is called the kilo in ordinary conversation.

You could get a rough idea of how heavy a kilogram is by filling the one-liter box mentioned in the preced-

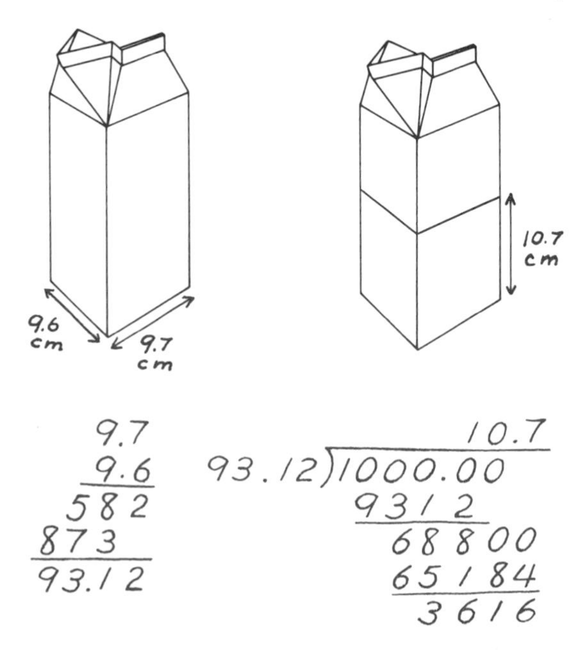

ing chapter with water. However, cardboard soaks up water quickly, and when it does, it bends out of shape, and this changes the volume of the box and hence the weight of the water it can hold. A better idea is to use an empty milk carton. If you use a one-quart carton, open the upper part completely so that all four sides are completely straight from top to bottom of the carton. If you use a larger size, you can cut the top away. Now draw a line on the side of the carton to indicate a volume of one liter. You can determine where this line should be by following this procedure:

1. Measure two adjacent sides of the bottom of the carton. Take the measurements in centimeters.
2. Multiply the length of one side by that of the other.
3. Divide your answer into 1,000 (because there are 1,000 $cm^3$ in a liter). The answer is the distance in centimeters that the line should be from the bottom of the carton.

Fill the carton to that line with water, and you will have a kilogram of water. Of course, when you pick it up, you will also have the weight of the carton in your hands, but that is a fairly small weight compared with that of the water.

The average person rarely has the occasion to weigh out just a few grams or milligrams, for the ordinary scales in our homes are not accurate enough to weigh objects that light. Yet it is surprising how many small items that we may use frequently have weights in the general range of grams or milligrams. Here are the approximate weights of some small, everyday items:

marble, 4.8 g

penny, 3.1 g

dime, 2.3 g

dollar bill, 1.1 g

paper clip, 560 mg

kernel of popping corn, 120 mg

split pea (half), 68 mg

postage stamp (2.2 × 2.5 cm), 64 mg

staple, 37 mg

flake of oatmeal, 25 mg

Of course, some of these items come in different sizes, and so other specimens might be somewhat heavier or lighter.

Table 10 summarizes some conversion factors of weight in the metric system. Table 11 summarizes some conversion factors of avoirdupois weight, which is the most common system used to weigh things in the United States. However, our system is further complicated by troy weight, which is used for weighing precious metals and gems, and apothecaries' weight, which has been used for weighing drugs (but pharmacists now use the metric system). The troy and apothecaries' pounds weigh 144/175 of an avoirdupois pound and are divided into twelve ounces. Again the metric system seems much simpler.

## TABLE 10

### Some Conversions of Units of Weight in the Metric System

| MEGAGRAMS[1] (Mg) | | KILOGRAMS (kg) | | GRAMS (g) |
|---|---|---|---|---|
| 1 Mg | = | 1,000 kg | = | 1,000,000 g |
| 0.001 Mg | = | 1 kg | = | 1,000 g |
| 0.000,001 Mg | = | 0.001 kg | = | 1 g |

[1] also called tonnes or metric tons

## TABLE 11

### Some Conversions of Units of Weight (Avoirdupois) in the Customary System

| SHORT TONS | | POUNDS (lb) | | OUNCES (oz) |
|---|---|---|---|---|
| 1 ton | = | 2,000 lb | = | 32,000 oz |
| $\frac{1}{2,000}$ ton | = | 1 lb | = | 16 oz |
| $\frac{1}{32,000}$ ton | = | $\frac{1}{16}$ lb | = | 1 oz |

# 6 Temperature and the Metric System

Two metric scales of temperature exist. One, the Kelvin scale, is the official SI scale, and it is used primarily by some scientists, especially chemists and physicists. The other, the Celsius scale, is used by ordinary people in their everyday lives, and many scientists use it as well.

The Celsius scale is named in honor of the Swedish astronomer, Anders Celsius, who devised it. The Celsius scale has also been called the centigrade scale, but the word centigrade has another meaning and is best not used to indicate temperature. (A grade is an angle that is one hundredth of a right angle. Can you tell, then, what a centigrade is?)

The upper case letter *C* was used to indicate a temperature given on the centigrade scale and is now used to indicate temperature on the Celsius scale.

On the Celsius scale, 0°C is set at the freezing point of water, and 100°C is set at the boiling point of water. Between them are 100 degrees (hence the older name, centigrade).

The Fahrenheit temperature scale, with which Americans are familiar, sets 32°F as equal to the freezing point of water and 212°F as equal to the boiling point of water. This means that there are 180 Fahrenheit degrees between the freezing and boiling points of

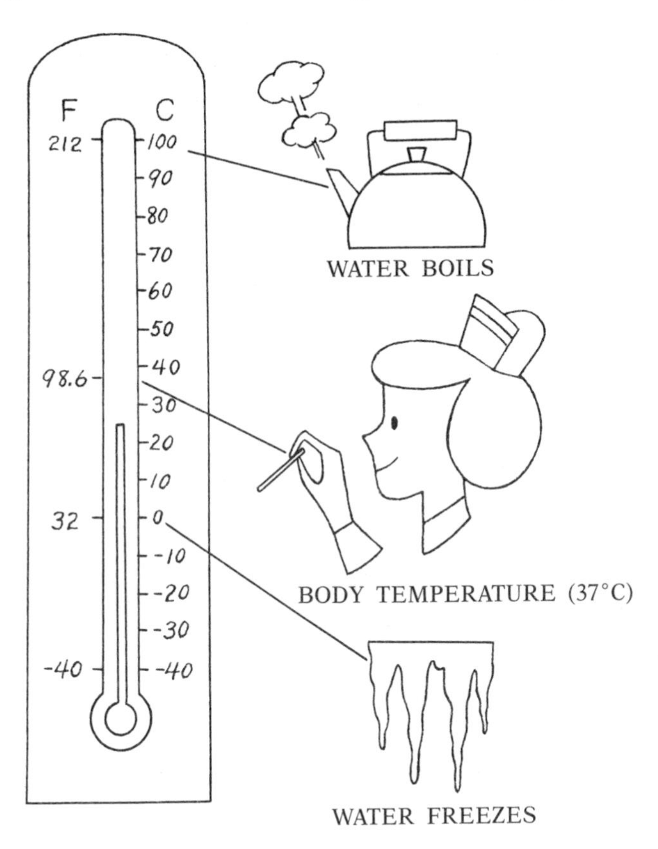

water. Therefore, a Celsius degree is larger than a Fahrenheit degree–1.8 times as large. If your doctor uses a Celsius thermometer and tells you your temperature is 2 degrees above normal, your condition is more serious than if he says the same thing after taking your temperature with a Fahrenheit thermometer.

You should become familiar with what a few temperatures on the Celsius scale indicate. A temperature of 0° is cold, for water freezes at this temperature, but 0°C is not so bitter cold as 0°F. Most refrigerators maintain a temperature of about 4°C. On a balmy spring day the temperature might be 15° or 20°C. A comfortable room temperature ranges from about 20° to 22°C for most persons, though some may prefer

25°C. Normal human body temperature is 37°C; this temperature outdoors is quite uncomfortably warm for nearly everyone.

You can easily become more familiar with the Celsius scale by using a Celsius thermometer. Keep one in your room or outdoors for a year. Read the temperature every time you pass the thermometer, and the Celsius scale will begin to mean more to you. If you cannot easily get a Celsius thermometer, perhaps you can get an inexpensive Fahrenheit thermometer. On a piece of paper or cardboard cut to the right size to fit the thermometer, put the following numbers so that they coincide with the numbers already on the thermometer and glue it on the Fahrenheit thermometer:

| °C | °F |
|---|---|
| –40 | –40 |
| –30 | –22 |
| –20 | – 4 |
| –10 | 14 |
| 0 | 32 |
| 10 | 50 |
| 20 | 68 |
| 30 | 86 |
| 40 | 104 |
| 50 | 122 |

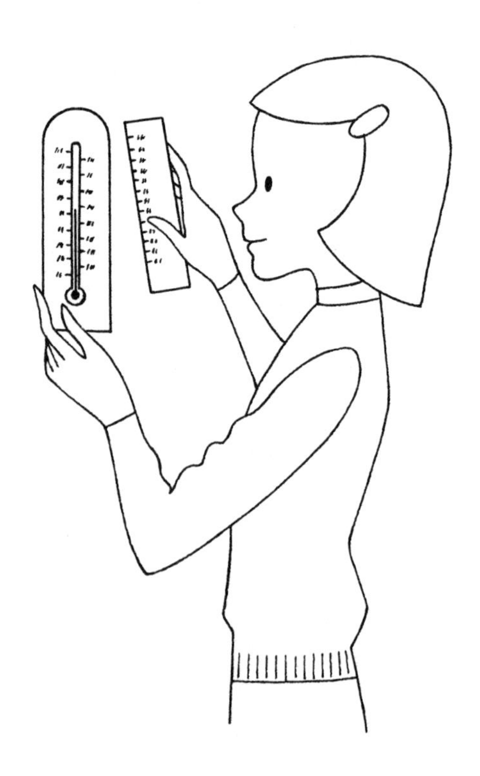

The new numbers will give you the temperature on the Celsius scale.

If you wish to continue to even higher temperatures do so by adding 10 Celsius degrees for each 18 Fahrenheit degrees. If your arithmetic is correct, 100°C will be opposite 212°F.

The Kelvin scale was devised so that 0°K would be the coldest temperature theoretically possible. Therefore, there are no temperatures below zero on the Kelvin scale as there are on the Celsius and Fahrenheit scales. Each degree on the Kelvin scale is called a kelvin and is equal to a Celsius degree. Because 0°K (also called absolute zero) is exactly 273.15 below zero on the Celsius scale, a given temperature on the Kelvin scale is always 273.15 degrees higher than it is on the Celsius scale.

You may have to become familiar with the Kelvin scale in some science classes, but don't worry about the weatherman predicting the temperature in degrees Kelvin.

# 7 *Time and the Metric System*

The second is the base unit of time in SI, and it probably is the only metric unit of time that most of us ordinarily will use. The second once was defined as $^1/_{86,400}$ of a mean (average) solar day. A mean solar day was chosen because the length of a "24-hour" day changes throughout the year—some days being slightly longer than 24 hours, others slightly shorter. Using $^1/_{86,400}$ of a mean solar day as a second would not be so bad, but the rotation of the earth on its axis is slowing down, and this makes the days longer—not enough that the ordinary person would notice it, but enough to cause error in precise work.

Today the second is defined in terms of the duration of the period of radiation emitted by a cesium atom undergoing a particular energy change (see Appendix for a more precise definition).

A second is a very short period of time, and most of us would rarely want to use submultiples of the second. If you blink four times in one second each blink requires about 250 milliseconds, but few ordinary persons are interested in measuring anything of so short a duration as a blink. Some scientists, on the other hand, do find it necessary to time events of much shorter duration.

Most of us are not likely to find the multiples of the second convenient to use either, for none of them coincides with natural periods of time like a day or year. A kilosecond, for instance, is 16 minutes 40 seconds, and a megasecond is a little more than eleven and a half days. It certainly seems convenient to retain the day as a unit of time even though it is not part of the metric system. There is nothing natural about the minute or the hour, but as long as days and years do not coincide with the metric system, there probably would be little gained by devising metric minutes and hours.

Our present system of reckoning time probably will be unchanged when we adopt the metric system. It is unlikely that the average person will think of the hour as 3.6 kiloseconds or the year as approximately 31.5 megaseconds.

# 8 *The Metric System in Use*

Some Americans become worried when they read that a yard equals 0.914 meter, a liquid quart equals 0.946 liter and one pound equals 454 grams. Perhaps they anticipate having to purchase cloth by the 0.914 meter, milk by the 0.946 liter, or butter by 454 grams. That, of course, is ridiculous. When we adopt the metric system, we will buy cloth by the even meter, milk will be sold in cartons that hold a liter, and a package of butter will weigh 500 grams (0.5 kilograms). Once the metric system is adopted there should be less and less reason to convert from customary to metric units or from metric to customary. Eventually, all the conversions that anyone would want to do would be within the metric system itself, and we have already

seen how easy that is. Should you be interested in conversions between the metric and customary systems, the table in the Appendix will be useful to you.

It will take a little time to become used to the metric system in many aspects of life. A roadside sign saying 80 km per hour may be a little startling until you realize that the speed limit is the same as the more familiar 50 miles per hour. With time, however, we will think of that speed in terms of 80 kilometers per hour rather than 50 miles per hour. A beauty contest winner whose

measurements are 91—63—91 is not unusually plump if those measurements are in centimeters. Perhaps she weighs 50 kg.

There may be some areas of life in which we prefer not to convert to the metric system. Will a football field become larger because it is measured in meters instead of yards? Or will we keep the field as it is, yards and all? Retaining the customary system in a special case like this would not be unusual. After all, the distance run by horses in some races is still measured in furlongs, a unit of measurement equal to $\frac{1}{8}$ of a mile and unfamiliar to most persons not interested in horseracing. The height of horses is also measured in hands. A hand,

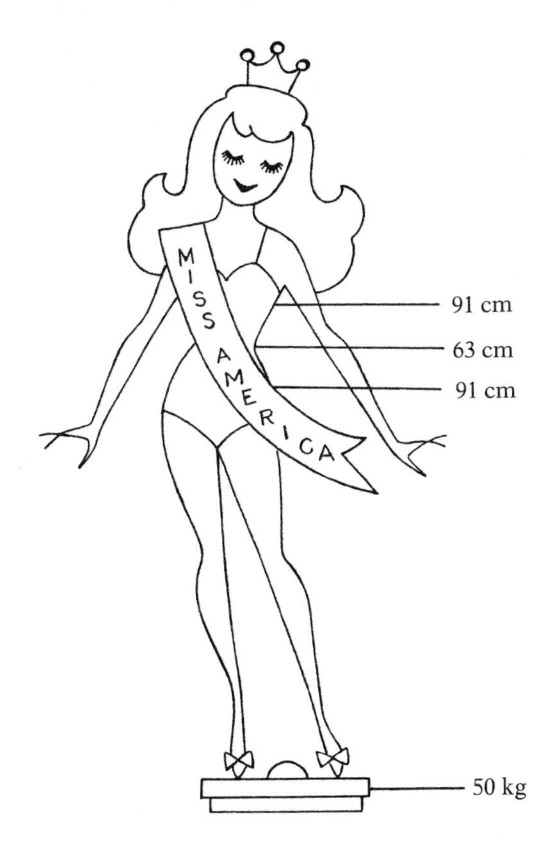

which is equal to 4 inches, is probably an unfamiliar unit to most persons.

In our private lives sometimes we will choose not to convert to the metric system. A cook can just as easily keep her old measuring cups and spoons and prepare dishes from her favorite recipes without making a conversion from one system to another. But she will want to have metric measuring cups and spoons to use with recipes in new cookbooks.

Young persons in school, however, soon may learn only the metric system. Even today, many pupils are taught both the metric and the customary systems in school, and in some of these schools, the metric system is taught as the more important of the two. We hope that soon people in every country will be familiar with the metric system. Then, even though some persons may prefer to use another system privately or for some special purpose, everyone will understand the one international system—the metric system.

# Appendix

# SI BASE UNITS, SUPPLEMENTARY UNITS, AND DERIVED UNITS

| QUANTITY | UNIT | SYMBOL | FORMULA |
|---|---|---|---|
| *Base Units:* | | | |
| length | meter | m | . . . |
| mass | kilogram | kg | . . . |
| time | second | s | . . . |
| electric current | ampere | A | . . . |
| thermodynamic temperature | kelvin | K | . . . |
| luminous intensity | candela | cd | . . . |
| amount of substance | mole | mol | . . . |
| *Supplementary Units:* | | | |
| plane angle | radian | rad | . . . |
| solid angle | steradian | sr | . . . |
| *Derived Units:* | | | |
| acceleration | meter per second squared | . . . | $m/s^2$ |
| activity (of a radioactive source) | disintegration per second | . . . | (disintegration)/s |
| angular acceleration | radian per second squared | . . . | $rad/s^2$ |
| angular velocity | radian per second | . . . | rad/s |
| area | square meter | . . . | $m^2$ |
| density | kilogram per cubic meter | . . . | $kg/m^3$ |
| electric capacitance | farad | F | A·s/V |
| electrical conductance | siemens | S | A/V |
| electric field strength | volt per meter | . . . | V/m |
| electric inductance | henry | H | V·s/A |
| electric potential difference | volt | V | W/A |
| electric resistance | ohm | Ω | V/A |
| electromotive force | volt | V | W/A |
| energy | joule | J | N·m |
| entropy | joule per kelvin | . . . | J/K |
| force | newton | N | $kg \cdot m/s^2$ |
| frequency | hertz | Hz | (cycle)/s |
| illuminance | lux | lx | $lm/m^2$ |
| luminance | candela per square meter | . . . | $cd/m^2$ |

| | | | |
|---|---|---|---|
| luminous flux | lumen | lm | cd·sr |
| magnetic field strength | ampere per meter | . . . | A/m |
| magnetic flux | weber | Wb | V·s |
| magnetic flux density | tesla | T | $Wb/m^2$ |
| magnetomotive force | ampere | A | . . . |
| power | watt | W | J/s |
| pressure | pascal | Pa | $N/m^2$ |
| quantity of electricity | coulomb | C | A·s |
| quantity of heat | joule | J | N·m |
| radiant intensity | watt per steradian | . . . | W/sr |
| specific heat | joule per kilogram-kelvin | . . . | J/kg·K |
| stress | pascal | Pa | $N/m^2$ |
| thermal conductivity | watt per meter-kelvin | . . . | W/m·K |
| velocity | meter per second | . . . | m/s |
| viscosity, dynamic | pascal-second | . . . | Pa·s |
| viscosity, kinematic | square meter per second | . . . | $m^2/s$ |
| voltage | volt | V | W/A |
| volume | cubic meter | . . . | $m^3$ |
| wavenumber | reciprocal meter | . . . | (wave)/m |
| work | joule | J | N·m |

## DEFINITIONS OF SI BASE UNITS

The meter is the length equal to 1,650,763.73 wavelengths in vacuum of the radiation corresponding to the transition between the levels $2p_{10}$ and $5d_5$ of the krypton-86 atom.

The kilogram is the unit of mass; it is equal to the mass of the international prototype of the kilogram.

The second is the duration of 9,192,631,770 periods of the radiation corresponding to the transition between the two hyperfine levels of the ground state of the cesium-133 atom.

The ampere is that constant current which, if maintained in two straight parallel conductors of infinite length, of negligible cross section, and placed one meter apart in vacuum, would produce between these conductors a force equal to $2 \times 10^{-7}$ newton per meter of length.

The kelvin, a unit of thermodynamic temperature, is the fraction $1/273.16$ of the thermodynamic temperature of the triple point of water.

The candela is the luminous intensity, in the perpendicular direction, of a surface of $1/600,000$ square meter of a blackbody at the temperature of freezing platinum under a pressure of 101,325 newtons per square meter.

The mole is the amount of substance of a system which contains as many elementary entities as there are atoms in 0.012 kilogram of carbon-12.

## DEFINITIONS OF SI SUPPLEMENTARY UNITS

The radian is the unit of measure of a plane angle with its vertex at the center of a circle and subtended by an arc equal in length to the radius.

The steradian is the unit of measure of a solid angle with its vertex at the center of a sphere and enclosing an area of the spherical surface equal to that of a square with sides equal in length to the radius.

## DEFINITIONS OF SI DERIVED UNITS WITH SPECIAL NAMES

| QUANTITY | UNIT AND DEFINITION |
|---|---|
| Electrical capacitance | The *farad* is the capacitance of a capacitor between the plates of which there appears a difference of potential of one volt when it is charged by a quantity of electricity equal to one coulomb. |
| Electrical conductance | The *siemens* is the electrical conductance of a conductor in which a current of one ampere is produced by an electric potential difference of one volt. |
| Electric inductance | The *henry* is the inductance of a closed circuit in which an electromotive force of one volt is produced when the electric current in the circuit varies uniformly at a rate of one ampere per second. |
| Electric potential difference (electromotive force) | The *volt* (unit of electric potential difference and electromotive force) is the difference of electric potential between two points of a conductor carrying a constant current of one ampere, when the power dissipated between these points is equal to one watt. |
| Electric resistance | The *ohm* is the electric resistance between two points of a conductor when a constant difference of potential of one volt, applied between these two points, produces in this conductor a current of one ampere, this conductor not being the source of any electromotive force. |

| | |
|---|---|
| Energy | The *joule* is the work done when the point of application of a force of one newton is displaced a distance of one meter in the direction of the force. |
| Force | The *newton* is that force which, when applied to a body having a mass of one kilogram gives it an acceleration of one meter per second per second. |
| Frequency | The *hertz* is a frequency of one cycle per second. |
| Illuminance | The *lux* is the illuminance produced by a luminous flux of one lumen uniformly distributed over a surface of one square meter. |
| Luminous flux | The *lumen* is the luminous flux emitted in a solid angle of one steradian by a point source having a uniform intensity of one candela. |
| Magnetic flux | The *weber* is the magnetic flux which, linking a circuit of one turn, produces in it an electromotive force of one volt as it is reduced to zero at a uniform rate in one second. |
| Magnetic flux density | The *tesla* is the magnetic flux density given by a magnetic flux of one weber per square meter. |
| Power | The *watt* is the power which gives rise to the production of energy at the rate of one joule per second. |
| Pressure or stress | The *pascal* is the pressure or stress of one newton per square meter. |
| Quantity of electricity | The *coulomb* is the quantity of electricity transported in one second by a current of one ampere. |

## HOW TO USE EXPONENTS

Numbers are part of our lives. Most of us usually do not work with very large numbers or very small numbers, but everyone should be ready to do so. The use of exponents can make the handling of such numbers somewhat easier. You don't have to understand exponents to be able to use the metric system. You can skip this part of the Appendix and still be able to buy a kilogram of hamburger in the supermarket. However, you might find the explanation of exponents interesting.

Let us suppose that a biologist is working with bacteria. Bacteria are microscopic living things, and a great many of them can occupy even one drop of water. If the biologist has a test tube that contains 10,000,000,000 bacteria and a flask that contains 1,000,000,000,000 bacteria, which has more bacteria, the test tube or the flask? The two numbers are large and a little awkward, and you must pause to count the zeros to tell which is the larger.

The use of exponents in a case like this may make the question a little easier to answer. An exponent indicates how many times a number is multiplied by itself, and the exponent is written as a small superscript immediately following that number. For instance,

$$10 \times 10 = 100 = 10^2$$
$$10 \times 10 \times 10 = 1{,}000 = 10^3$$
$$10 \times 10 \times 10 \times 10 = 10{,}000 = 10^4$$

In these examples, 2, 3, and 4 are exponents of ten. Using these examples again, we say that 100, 1,000, and 10,000 are powers of 10: 100 is the second power of 10; 1,000 is the third power of 10; and 10,000 is the fourth power of 10.

You can see that for a given power of 10, the appropriate exponent of 10 can be determined easily by adding the zeros in the number. For instance, 1,000 which has three zeros, equals $10^3$. Then the 10,000,000,000 bacteria in the test tube can be indicated as $10^{10}$ bacteria, and the 1,000,000,000,000 bacteria become $10^{12}$. If the numbers of bacteria in the original problem had been written this way, we could have determined at a glance that the flask contains more bacteria than the test tube.

Exponents can be used to express decimal fractions, too. One of the bacteria might have a length of 0.000,001 meter—another figure awkward to persons not accustomed to using such small numbers. (Of course, we might find it more convenient to say that a bacterium is 1.0 micrometer long, but for the moment let's stick with 0.000,001 meter.) If we were to begin a list of powers of ten beginning with those we have already mentioned and continuing down to smaller powers of 10, we would see that 10 itself equals $10^1$, 1 equals $10^0$, and decimal powers of 10 have negative exponents:

$$\begin{aligned} 10{,}000 &= 10^4 \\ 1{,}000 &= 10^3 \\ 100 &= 10^2 \\ 10 &= 10^1 \\ 1 &= 10^0 \\ 0.1 &= 10^{-1} \\ 0.01 &= 10^{-2} \\ 0.001 &= 10^{-3} \\ 0.000{,}1 &= 10^{-4} \end{aligned}$$

In the case of decimal powers of 10, the exponent is equal to *one more* than the number of zeros after the decimal point and then receives a negative sign. A measurement of 0.000,001 meter is expressed exponentially as $10^{-6}$ meter. It might be just a little easier to see that $10^{-5}$ is larger than $10^{-6}$ (remember that $-5$ is larger than $-6$) than it is to see that 0.000,01 is larger than 0.000,001.

Of course, only a few numbers consist of a 1 and several zeros before or after it. Take 2,500 as an example. Is there a way we can express this number exponentially? Yes, and the following is one way:

$$\begin{aligned} \text{If } 2{,}500 &= 2.5 \times 1{,}000 \\ \text{then } 2{,}500 &= 2.5 \times 10^3 \end{aligned}$$

Or, if you wish, because $2{,}500 = 25 \times 100$

$$\text{then } 2{,}500 = 25 \times 10^2$$

$$\begin{array}{r} 2.5 \times 10^3 \\ \times \quad 3 \times 10^2 \\ \hline 7.5 \times 10^5 \end{array}$$

If you like, check by multiplying in the ordinary way:

$$\begin{array}{r} 2{,}500 \\ \times \quad 300 \\ \hline 750{,}000 \end{array} = 7.5 \times 100{,}000 = 7.5 \times 10^5$$

DIVISION WITH EXPONENTS. Division is accomplished by subtracting exponents. If you want to determine how much larger is the bacterial population in the flask than the one in the test tube, you would divide the size of the larger population by the size of the smaller population. Set up in the ordinary way, the problem is:

$$\frac{1{,}00\not0{,}\not0\not0\not0{,}\not0\not0\not0{,}\not0\not0\not0}{1\not0{,}\not0\not0\not0{,}\not0\not0\not0{,}\not0\not0\not0}$$

by cancelling out a lot of zeros

$$\frac{1{,}000{,}000{,}000{,}000}{10{,}000{,}000{,}000}$$

you would arrive at $\frac{100}{1} = 100.$

A simpler method is to subtract exponents:

$$\frac{10^{12}}{10^{10}} = 10^2 \text{ (which equals 100)}$$

After all, that is all you really were doing in the more laborious cancelling out of zeros—you took 10 zeros away from the 12 zeros in 1,000,000,000,000.

In the slightly more complex example of dividing 420,000

by 600, change 420,000 to $4.2 \times 10^5$ and 600 to $6 \times 10^2$ and set up the problem:

$$\frac{420{,}000}{600} = \frac{4.2 \times 10^5}{6 \times 10^2}$$

Now divide 4.2 by 6 in the ordinary way and divide $10^5$ by $10^2$ by subtracting exponents:

$$\frac{4.2 \times 10^5}{6 \times 10^2} = 0.7 \times 10^3 \text{ or } 7 \times 10^2$$

ADDITION AND SUBTRACTION WITH EXPONENTS. The use of exponents does not make addition and subtraction any easier. It probably is more bothersome, if anything. However, you might want to know how to do it.

In adding or subtracting exponential figures, you must be sure that all of the figures to be added have the same exponent. You cannot add $10^3$ and $10^2$ directly. Convert one into terms of the other. For example:

$$\begin{array}{rcr} 10^3 & = & 10 \times 10^2 \\ +10^2 & = & +\ 1 \times 10^2 \\ \hline & & 11 \times 10^2 \end{array}$$

Notice that in the actual addition, the exponent does not change—that is, the exponents themselves are not added. If you wish to check the procedure by the ordinary way:

$$\begin{array}{rcl} 10^3 & = & 1{,}000 \\ +10^2 & = & +\ 100 \\ \hline & & 1{,}100 \text{ (which equals } 11 \times 10^2\text{)} \end{array}$$

A subtraction problem is set up similarly. To subtract $6 \times 10^3$ from $3 \times 10^4$:

$$\begin{array}{rcl} 3 \times 10^4 & = & 30 \times 10^3 \\ -6 \times 10^3 & = & -6 \times 10^3 \\ \hline & & 24 \times 10^3 \text{ (which equals } 2.4 \times 10^4\text{)} \end{array}$$

As in addition, the exponents themselves do not change in the subtraction itself.

Similarly, because $2{,}500 = 0.25 \times 10{,}000$

$$\text{then } 2{,}500 = 0.25 \times 10^4$$

Ordinarily we would write 2,500 as $2.5 \times 10^3$ (that is, as a number between 1 and 10 multiplied by the correct power of 10), but if there is a reason to change it to another expression, you are free to do so.

MULTIPLICATION WITH EXPONENTS. Exponents not only make some numbers less difficult to understand, they also can make multiplication easier. One way of multiplying $1{,}000 \times 100$ is to set up the problem this way:

$$\begin{array}{r} 1{,}000 \\ \times\ \ 100 \\ \hline 100{,}000 \end{array}$$

Your answer contains a string of zeros equal to all the zeros in 1,000 and 100. A simpler way is to multiply by adding exponents:

$$\begin{array}{l} \ \ 10^3 \\ \times 10^2 \\ \hline \ \ 10^5 \text{ (which equals 100,000)} \end{array}$$

A multiplication problem can be a little more complicated, say $2{,}500 \times 300$. In this case you would change 2,500 to $2.5 \times 10^3$ as we did above, and change 300 (which equals $3 \times 100$) to $3 \times 10^2$. Now set up your multiplication problem:

$$\begin{array}{r} 2.5 \times 10^3 \\ \times\ \ 3 \times 10^2 \\ \hline \end{array}$$

then multiply $2.5 \times 3$ in the ordinary way and multiply $10^3 \times 10^2$ by adding exponents:

## THE CONCEPT OF MASS

The concept of mass is often confused with that of weight, but the two terms do not mean the same thing. Mass refers to the quantity of matter and is expressed in kilograms. In everyday conditions on earth, we can use the terms mass and weight more or less interchangeably; but while the mass of something does not change, its weight can, for the weight of matter depends partly on the gravitational pull to which it is subjected.

Our units of weight are standardized with those of mass so that under the gravitational pull at the surface of the earth, an object with a mass of one kilogram weighs one kilogram. On the moon, in space, or on another planet, that bit of matter would still have a mass of one kilogram, but it would have a different weight. During the space program involving trips to the moon, television viewers became familiar with the sight of an astronaut hopping easily on the moon and floating effortlessly in space. This is because the astronaut weighed only one-sixth of his earth weight while on the moon (which has one-sixth the gravitational pull of the earth), and he was weightless in space. Under all these conditions his mass did not change; he still consisted of the same quantity of matter (except for some minor temporary inequality in the amount of food and oxygen he used compared with the wastes he produced).

# Conversion Factors

# SOME CONVERSION FACTORS BETWEEN THE METRIC AND CUSTOMARY SYSTEMS

| *Metric to Customary* | *Customary to Metric* |
|---|---|
| **LENGTH** | |
| 1 kilometer = 0.621371 mile | 1 mile = 1.609344 kilometer |
| 1 meter = 1.09361 yards = 39.3701 inches | 1 yard = 0.9144 meter |
| 1 decimeter = 0.328084 foot | 1 foot = 3.048 decimeters = 30.48 centimeters |
| 1 centimeter = 0.393701 inch | 1 inch = 2.54 centimeters = 25.4 millimeters |
| **AREA** | |
| 1 square kilometer = 0.386102 square mile | 1 square mile = 2.589988 square kilometers |
| 1 square meter = 1.19599 square yards | 1 square yard = 0.8361274 square meter |
| = 10.7639 square feet | 1 square foot = 9.290304 square decimeters |
| 1 square centimeter = 0.155 square inch | = 929.0304 square centimeters |
| | 1 square inch = 6.4516 square centimeters |

## VOLUME

1 cubic meter (1 kiloliter) = 1.30795 cubic yards
1 cubic decimeter (1 liter)
 = 1.05669 quarts (U.S. liquid)
 = 0.908083 quart (U.S. dry)
1 cubic centimeter (1 milliliter)
 = 0.202884 teaspoon

1 gallon (U.S. liquid) = 3.785412 liters
1 quart (U.S. liquid) = 0.943529 liter
1 quart (U.S. dry) = 1.101221 liters
1 pint (U.S. liquid) = 0.473165 liter
1 pint (U.S. dry) = 0.5506105 liter
1 cup = 0.2365882 liter
1 tablespoon = 14.78676 milliliters
1 teaspoon = 4.928922 milliliters
1 bushel = 35.23907 liters
1 peck = 8.809768 liters
1 cubic yard = 0.7645549 cubic meter
1 cubic foot = 28.31685 cubic decimeters (liters)
1 cubic inch = 16.387064 cubic centimeters

## WEIGHT

1 megagram (metric ton, tonne)
 = 1.102311 short tons
1 kilogram = 2.20462 pounds (avoirdupois)
1 gram = 0.035274 ounces (avoirdupois)

1 short ton = 0.9071847 megagram
1 pound (avoirdupois) = 453.5924 grams
1 ounce (avoirdupois) = 28.34952 grams

## TEMPERATURE

$$°F = (°C \times 1.8) + 32$$

$$°C = \frac{°F - 32}{1.8}$$